THE FUTURE AHEAD

War & Willingness to Live

Why did I Fear Death When None Vares?

WUR DENG LUETH

THE FUTURE AHEAD

Copyright © 2022 by Wur Deng Lueth

All rights reserved. No part of this publication may be reproduced, distributed, or transmitted in any form or by any means, including photocopying, recording, or other electronic or mechanical methods, without the prior written permission of the publisher, except in the case of brief quotations embodied in critical reviews and certain other noncommercial uses permitted by copyright law.

CONTENTS

INTRODUCTION 1
ACKNOWLEDGMENTS 7
CHAPTER 1 At the Beginning 9
CHAPTER 2 My Journey to Khartoum 20
CHAPTER 3 My identity, culture, value, and enemies 29
CHAPTER 4 A peaceful city for all 36
CHAPTER 5 Those who die on the front line and behind the war 51
CHAPTER 6 I wish God could change the circumstances 56
CHAPTER 7 I was born black and became black by society's definition 66
CHAPTER 8 Long-suffering, and no ending soon 71
CHAPTER 9 How far I have come Up to this point in my life's journey 78
CHAPTER 10 The End 88

THE FUTURE AHEAD BOOK

The Future Ahead is a book that tells the story of my life journey from a small town to the capital city. I left my birthplace at the beginning of the year 1985 when all our belongings were burned down and destroyed. That year was the genesis of my life's uncertain journey; my parents had to make difficult choices. Death, as a result of hunger or being killed in the war, was more magnificent than life. The survival rate was close to zero since we had no weapons to defend our city. The only option for my parents was to send us away—the love parents give their children to have a future. So, my father sent my older brother and I to North Sudan. It was not an easy decision, but it was safer than staying in the South. My journey started with just one decision, which has kept me alive till today. A man cannot live a peaceful and happy life or survive without having a great inner imagination. Our lives partially rely on internal dialogs, and the quality of vision and dialogues can make a difference in our world. There are choices to be made in every situation, and without internal creation, nothing would exist in the physical form. My father will be my hero for the rest of my life. His decision to send me away to survive the war and have a life and the future ahead is priceless. Leaving my hometown was a new beginning. It was like having a blind date with my own life; I didn't know where I was going and had no map or path to follow. As the journey began, I had to face the reality of life on the road I rode on alone. You might ask, why should I care to read this book? Because it is a war story, war brings two things: death and unpleasant experiences. I did end up in the United States of America because of the civil war in Sudan. So, knowing what other parts of the world are experiencing is beneficial to how you view the world.

About The Book

The goal is to inspire young children, especially ones who do not have parents. The book is about my personal story and the life lessons I have learned while moving from my hometown to Sudan's capital, then to the United States of America as an immigrant. The journey to North Sudan results from the civil war in the early 80s. The book consists of ten chapters; each chapter comprises other branches. There is no logical order, but it begins from my childhood memories, experiences, and lessons learned, and as you will read through, it seems like opinions. But the greater portion is about my experience over the course of my life journey and building a belief lens through which I see the world. The book's weakness is its partial experiences due to the lack of visiting the whole world, city, or state, as I was limited to the number of places I could see and limited to the number of people I could interact with. Sudan had its independence in 1956, and afterward, a civil war broke out between the North and the South.

What In The Book

What you will read in the book

- ➤ My childhood - my birthplace included
- ➤ Growing up in a Dinka tribe - norms and cultures that the society expects you to conform to.
- ➤ Having the same value and behavior as a requirement - this uniformity norm prevents the growth of the individual.
- ➤ Dinka Tribe (Jieng) values, culture, and marriage laws.
  - The norms allow immediate relatives if you die to marry on your behalf or if you cannot independently.
  - I was the last child of five boys, but three of my brothers and my parents are no longer with us because of war.
  - Beginning my education journey and whose idea it was for joining the school.
  - What were the challenges of joining the school?
- ➤ A war that forced me to leave my family behind
  - In early 1985
  - Sudan's Civil War
  - A war that affected lives and development
  - The conflict was a result of ignorance

- ➢ Awareness and knowledge create a necessity for change—and silence was no longer an option
  - When we learn facts, new light shines the way to change.
- ➢ The lessons I have learned and experienced from my journey up to this time— School, work, religions, and my interactions with people.
- ➢ My identity and its enemies
  - Stepping into a new identity
- ➢ A new chapter of my life began with one decision.
  - In beginning
  - My father decided to send us away from the village, hoping we could have a future one day. And I have learned that good things come and go, by choice or no choice. I think my story is worth sharing because it will benefit and encourage children and young adults who have lost their loved ones to reach their dream, see things differently, and overcome their challenges. By having hope and believing everything is possible, if you keep trying, you will surely arrive at your desired destination.

The Lessons I Have Learned

The lesson I have learned as I move from city to city is that I was born black. Blackness goes beyond skin color; it is how you perceive in all aspects of life. It is embedded in human consciousness and reflected in daily interaction with others. Mistreatment and consciousness biases only apply to black skin color, and what happened in the past left a dark image and wrong perception about black people. These experiences trail me to all cities I have been to.

These biases only apply to our skin and past leftover dark images that shadow and trail us all over the earth. I have been to many classrooms, workplaces, and cities, but no difference to celebrate. Only you can help, treat, respect, and value you.

The Purpose Of This Book.

The book focuses on three areas of my life: my early childhood, my experiences, and the lessons I have learned in my journey up to this moment. This story is not opinions or complaints, but the story of my life journey during the civil war in Sudan. Also, it is the lessons I have learned as I moved from city to city and the impacts the war forced on us (the people of South Sudan). I'm sharing with you my story, and chances are, you may not have heard of or experienced the war against unbelievers or Christians. It still exists in this part of the world, even now, as I will share my experiences. Many questions came to my mind when I tried to understand the religious justification for wars started by the government of Sudan and the world as a whole. The civil war in Sudan gave a realistic view of the world we live in, that no one cares. Therefore, only you can help you. My parent's decision to send us away from our birthplace to make the future is the reason I'm here today, sharing my story with you. The second war resumed, presumably, in 1983. But at the beginning of 1984, the Sudan government began to attack cities and villages in South Sudan. Soon, the South became a war zone and was no longer useful for human inhabitation. People were dying from hunger as a result of the government burning down houses along with food. We would hide from soldiers in trees. Eventually, the soldiers learned how to navigate within bushes to find people and began shooting their guns in the forest. Also, they had cars we did not have. And the question was, when will you die? Feeling and experiencing your death was not easy at all, and fear had reached the highest level. As we faced these challenges, we didn't know if we would survive or not. I wondered if a God exists and what part of human life He's protecting or concerned with. Some may argue that all these are acts of the devil, but why did God create evil in the first place? We can go on asking endless questions with no real answers about why animals die even though they've not sinned. It was the darkest time in my life; the probability of me making it alive at that time was close to zero. Death was the natural, closer option since it was the enemy's goal— to kill non-Muslims or unbelievers. By far, the world operates on a power mode where the powerful remain on top and the weak remains at the bottom. You may experience unfairness whether you work at a coffee shop or for an enterprise business; the rules are set to serve only the one that made them. A robust stand on top of the weak prevents the more helpless from seeking a dram or seeing the world. You do not have to watch the news; you can experience it all in your daily interaction with others—and action only counts in life. My new life chapter began in early 1985; my brother and I were able to escape to north Sudan, leaving behind our parents and three other brothers forever.

ACKNOWLEDGMENTS

MY LIFE JOURNEY'S HEROES

Many people have contributed directly and indirectly to my life's journey, personal life, education, and work, and I owe each one of them gratitude. I am so grateful for all the impact you have had on my life; words are not enough to say thank you for all you've done for me. Abraham Gama was the first person to enroll me in a school when I moved to North Sudan. He was also the manager at my first job, where I worked as an office coffee boy. He gave me books, clothes, and shoes every year during my primary and middle school. Mayo Catholic Church also helped me during my high school years. My education and work lives began together during my primary and middle school. I would work in the morning and go to school at noon until 1992 when I was accepted into a boarding high school. My education almost came to an end since I could not afford to be a full-time student. Luckily, I was an active member of the church, the Mayo Catholic Church, South

Khartoum. At the time, I participated in many activities, including second reading on Sunday and wall youth writing articles, so I met Father John. He agreed to give me 100 Sudanese pounds every month for the three years of my high school years. Also, during my community college days, my supervisor at the target store would allow me to take every Wednesday morning off in order to go to school and do my homework. And IVY tech community writing center helps me in writing classes/my advisor professor Purdue University-Indianapolis School of engineering and technology. There are so many great people in my life, and I say thank you all for your kindness—you are my life heroes.

CHAPTER 1
AT THE BEGINNING

Until then…
I refuse to be a slave or poor in my soul.
I have endless joy that occupies my soul
—I cannot explain it, but I can feel it.
I love it!
I was here before my physical presence.
MY life and existence are continuity of the past.
I am a billionaire in my soul, and it is an abundance I experience
My human attributes are of higher quality.
I think as intended by the creator.
Too far-reaching
Too close reaching
The creator is closer as too far from us

Nowhere ending

Resources provider.

I refuse to be a slave or poor in soul.

I am the energy of unlimited power; therefore, I am no slave.

You, and I, and everyone else are here by the same channel that imagined all souls into existence.

I deny any command that does not respect my humanity. Therefore, no one can be my master now and forever.

Call it God, and I call it the provider.

In the end, I love you all.

My Birthplace

I was born in a small town called Pariang, which is now the capital of Ruweng State, after South Sudan gained independence from Sudan in 2011. I was the last of five boys. Three of my brothers were killed in the civil war between the South and North. Pariang town had one boarding primary school, Catholic churches, and hospitals. At that time, education was perceived as something for the poor and children who misbehave. Besides, the school was too far from the village, and it was the only boarding school. Students would stay in the school for almost a month before they were allowed to visit their homes. For these reasons, it was a challenge for the parents to approve of their children going to school. On the other hand, the wealthy family had their children stay at home to help them on the farm. The boys were trained to be cattle keepers; though my father had many cattle, our family was an exception—my parents could not communicate with my father's sister's son in English. That encouraged them to enroll one of my brothers in the school. In turn, my brother asked me to convince my father to allow me to go to school. So, one morning, sometime in June 1982, my father and I were on the farm when I asked him if he would allow me to join the school. He agreed and bought me a school uniform. That was my very first experience leaving my parents. My father would bring me milk every day. Two years after I left them forever, I lived in sadness every day. Sometimes, I would try to remember their images and what they looked like. I don't have an actual image of my parents, but I know both my parents are a tale. My mother was a tall black woman with white teeth. She was very kind. My father was a handsome, quiet, and wise man. My parents didn't deserve the death of the devil; this enemy had no soul at all, but it will remain the human enemy forever.

My Early Childhood Memories.

There are many memories of my childhood, but the best memory is the 'birds game.' My brother Chol and I used to play the 'birds game' in the rainy season. In the evening, we would sit facing the east and watch as different types of birds with different colors fly from the South to the North in a beautiful row, following one another as we choose a group of birds in shape, color, and size. We used to fight over birds flying in the sky; "These are mine," we would say. Another activity we used to do was toy making. There were no modern toys, so we made cow toys and other animals from the soil.

Early Childhood Education.

Wur was born in Pariang town in South Sudan. Wur went to Primary, middle, and high school in North Sudan at the beginning of the 80s. At an early age, he became interested in studying Electrical Engineering and Physics; he was accepted at Sudan University of Science and Technology - School of Electrical Engineering, 1995-1996. He then immigrated to the United States of America in 2004. He earned an Associate's degree in Computer Information Systems in 2010 from IVY TECH Community College in Indiana, a Bachelor's degree in Information Security from Purdue University in 2013, and a Master's degree in Network Security from DePaul University. He attended Capella University for a Doctor of Information Technology degree with a focus on Information Assurance and Cybersecurity, 2016-2018. Also, he loves reading, writing, and helping others; he's created a math and computer channel on YouTube, making learning accessible.

In The Beginning

By the beginning of 1984, Sudan had seen significant movement from South to North because of the civil war. When the war broke out, it started to spread all over the South. The war forced people to leave their villages and cities to either join the army forces that were fighting against the government of Sudan or run to other neighboring African countries. The South and the North were like two different countries in the sense that most people in the South speak English and other African languages, while Arabic is the official language spoken in the North. However, the economics vary, and the geographical distance between the South and North was not war-caused but was a conscious refusal to one another.

The North claims its origin, religion, beliefs, and language to Arabic roots. Opposite in the South claims African origin. In comparison, the North was more developed and stable than the South since all of Sudan's resources were deployed in the North by the government, causing inequality and unbalancing in the education system and power. It also resulted from the colonized policies against black African origin to keep Africa in the darkness, just as we witness today. Most Arabs still believe Africans are slaves or should be slaves. It's a collective responsibility for all Africans to show the world they are humans, just like the other races, and that they deserve respect and deserve to live. All the past wrongs against Africans were immoral and inhumane. I have great hope that one day, Africans will recover; sunlight will shine from east to west, and each individual will enjoy it equally. There was no job in the North. People were coming with no skills or experience, and some women had to clean the Arabs' houses. Some also made traditional wines to earn income

My Parent's Ethnicity

Both my parents are from the Dinka tribe (Jieng people). My father had three sisters; all of them were married, and that was my father's source of income and wealth, aside from my grandfather's cattle. My mother's brother was killed in tribe conflicts before I was born, so I grew up to be the cattle keeper. That was the primary career for men, especially the Jieng tribe because it provided food and marriage. You have to have a lot of cows and a good reputation before you can get married. Marriage in Dinka is similar to a loan you have to pay—you can pay immediately or later in life. As a mother, even if you die, your children will have to pay for your wedding, which is more than 300 cows. Love does not play a role in Dinka marriage; instead, the marriage is based on both families. After the marriage has taken place, they'll learn to build love. My life, in the beginning, seemed promising; all I needed to survive, respectfully, was available. My father and mother were wealthy in Jieng standard, which came with a reputation among the Jieng tribe. I could adapt in a reasonable manner and decide to marry whoever I wanted and live a simple life. A Dinka man usually marries at least two wives, and if a brother or close relative dies, you can marry their wives as well. The children carry their dead father. My father is my hero. I had freedom more than my others sibling did since I was the last child. I started my education in South Sudan, but I completed primary, middle school, and high school in North Sudan because of the war.

Early in my education journey, I became more interested in physics and electrical engineering.

I was admitted to Sudan University of Science and Technology, College of electrical engineering. I got my Sudan degree in 1995—I did not graduate. I then fell in love with technologies when I moved to the United States of America in 2004. I got my associate degree in Computer Information Systems in 2010 from Ivy Tech Community College. BS in Information Security from Purdue University, Indianapolis campus, MS from DePaul University, Chicago School of Computing, and digital media in Computer Network Information Security in 2015. I also attended Capella University for a Doctor of Information Technology degree in Information Assurance and Cybersecurity 2016-2018, but I did not graduate.

Immediate Help Was Needed But Was Nowhere To Turn.

In early 1984, Pariang and the surrounding areas were in a state of confusion and fear. The confusion came as a result of not knowing where to go or what to do, why we were being attacked, and not knowing which place was safe when the government was attacking us instead of protecting us. For the first time, I saw the military vehicles. I was helpless because the threat and risk of death were high, and I was willing to live; I wanted to see what the world had to offer. My will to live created fear, especially when God was nowhere to help, and there was no reason not to die. We needed help immediately, but there was nowhere to turn to. The civilians' challenges were so significant due to the inability to protect our lives from danger on all accounts and God being unresponsive to our plight. Sudan's civil war is the worst Africa has ever seen; millions of people died, as both God and the world were in deep silence or turned away from us. The war partly has religious aspects, exposing and forcing the people to the Islamic religion. The goal was to make South Sudan a gateway to Africa for the introduction to Arabicization. I wanted to continue living with my parents and brothers, but the choice to live in town was not ours to make. We wanted God to respond to our prayers immediately—and the hard part was, you don't even know if God is listening. The unbalancing power between the North and the South was incomparable, and only God could help, especially since we had no weapons to face the enemy. And the question always arises, what part of humans' life does God protect or is concerned about? The human soul's safety should be the core center of God's existence, especially when death comes with unwillingness. There was no food or water, and the world, including God, was far away to offer help to the South Sudan people. What I have learned and experienced is that the fact that we are black makes us undeserving of a good life or to even enjoying our human rights. The Sudan civil war will have a long-term impact on many generations to come because of the mass deaths and the crimes that the Sudan government committed against the people of the South. It has made peace-making between the North and the South impossible. The civil war itself could have been avoided, but the religious agenda toward us continued even after the South gained independence.

Slow Death
Khartoum Was A Place Of Slow Death

Finding meaning and purpose in life is difficult when the road to happiness and life is closed, and hope and reason for living as a human is lost. Khartoum was a place of slow death. As people came to the capital, there was no job or money to rent a house. People lived outside in open areas for a few months until the government created camps in displaced areas surrounding Khartoum. People wanted to live, but it was harder to get food to eat, and they had no skills to find work. That was the darkest time of my life. Life was not making any sense, making you ask where God was. Where was God in all this mess? Who is in control of all the things happening on earth? Some people may offer reason and explanation for all these, but when you are in a crisis and having difficulties, it is hard to believe there exists a loving God. People seek the meaning of life and get an impossible clear sense as to why our soul suffers. I want answers, but no one has an easy answer. Let me give you a real-life example, which is marriage as a symbol of love and unity. If you ask a married couple why they got married, you might hear what you do not expect to hear. And the reason is simple—we have different interests and desires for everything that has ever existed on earth, and it's for various reasons. These different needs have created an unstable world, and as a result, humans suffer physically. The soul is complicated and straightforward at the same time, and it provides us with power.

Each of us holds a different interest, which influences our decision-making, awareness, ignorance, and expectations. This phrase, "In the beginning," which can be found in the Bible, Old Testament, tells us that there was a beginning of the universe. This begs the question, what was before the beginning? And what was before the creation of the world we live in today? None for sure can give you pure and clear evidence without making reference to the same book that was written by the first human writers. Why did God create the world? I always wondered about the purpose of human existence; if there is a purpose and do what and for who? The purpose of life's existence could be a backward-thinking help of finding answers. An idea of the "beginning" makes you question so many things. For instance, if there was a beginning, was that before the start? Do you realize that humans do not do anything for God in all time we spend on earth? Try to revisit religious prayers and see if you can come across the phrase "God helped God" is all we do in life for human interest and welfare? We never understood why animals also die if human death is a result of the crime committed by the first humankind parents. When was the last time you took an exam where you never studied the contents, but you were expecting to pass?

With God, how you would have suffered—from God's goodness, one thing for sure—is that the creator has the power to make. But in a free fall, our fear projects and produces an imagined independent power; life is a delicate part of the energy that has a timestamp. The living could be in an endless existence. Living things might not hold meaningful value as we believe, and that omits the idea of living forever as not originally intended by the creator. Therefore, suffering and struggles may not center on the purposes and thoughtfulness of the sole provider. We cannot fulfill life and satisfy within without fulfilling social requirements, for example, education, awareness, confidence, and community association. Move we advance in life living interference our reality thinking -non-independent -fear - the result -Other or.

Define Your Own Language Of Life, Happiness, And Freedom

To live purposely, you have to define your own language of life and freedom—no one can give you the life that you want. Live life on your own terms; there is no wrong or right way—what you see in the world are behaviors and beliefs that seem to be accepted by society.

Life is an unstructured test you take every day; whether you pass or fail, you should learn from it. Try not to avoid taking it, so you can measure your ability. Be grateful for what you have today and what you will have tomorrow.

Live and be curious to learn more.
Live, learn, and experience as you move forward in life.
Live like it is critical; like when crossing the road,
it is crucial to look at both sides for your safety.
Live as you are, a human being on earth.

Define your language of freedom.

Live life and know your enemy.

Respect others for your well-being.

Live life and always seek wisdom.

*Live life and seek education not just to get paid
but also for your growth and society.*

Live life and seek understanding of others' points of view.

Seek love in the right places.

Live life, but know that no other has needs as you do.

Live life and seek wisdom even from your enemy.

Know that all living animals were born and that they have parents.

Correct your past mistake to discover a new opportunity.

Live meaningfully because life is not forever.

*Whether your life is prolonged, we all have an end;
and all we have is now.*

Finally, contribute to society as much as you can.

CHAPTER 2

MY JOURNEY TO KHARTOUM

On the new road, I go alone

The journey of uncertainty, I seek.

Sunrise, I will miss.

My parents, I will miss.

My brothers, I will miss.

The feeling of unsafety fills my bones.

New places, I will experience.

New people, I will meet and join.

The new world I will enter and be a part of.

New language, l will learn.

The fear of the enemy and the unknown world are the greatest.

A journey of uncertainty. Sometime in January 1985, the war forced me to leave my birthplace—and that was a new chapter of my life's journey. I had no idea where I was going; the event was out of my imagination. My only goal was to survive the war, but leaving my family behind was unimaginable—I had lost our togetherness, the sunrise, my birth city, and everything in-between forever. A new road I will ride on alone began. The new world has become a reality.

I was entering an unfamiliar world where I would meet new people and learn a new language. These were the challenges ahead of me. Running to North Sudan by myself would be suicidal. Our enemy's goal was to destroy us (our identity) and anything rooted in African culture or belief, and God failed to protect us. My question has always been, "what part of human life does God protect or concern Himself with?" Is He natural? Does He have a soul, feelings, or emotions, and does He even exist?

Most of all, does he even think about Black people?

> "Do unto others as you would have them do unto you."
> Give me peace, and I will worship you.
> Give me life, and I will worship you.
> Stop our enemies from killing us, and I will worship you.
> "You said to ask, seek, and it will be given unto us."

I asked, and I am still asking, that you protect our souls, just like other races.

I have seen enough, and that shows me you exist.

Today, most Southerners have converted to Islam—Arab names, culture, and women bleach their skins to be relevant. They hate and kill themselves, losing their national identity. These were no accidents, but Sudanese Arabs plan to destroy us and take over our resources. I learned from my experiences that African people, black-skinned people, in particular, have advantages. Their peaceful nature is being taken advantage of. When you are a gentle person, you do not expect bad to be you tourist everything, including humans and God. But in the world we live in, you have to create tools and gain knowledge to help others and protect yourself. In the past, if you are morally good, you don't need the protection of the military or police in society. In the beginning, there were five boys, including me.

History records our names.

The wisdom within and the freedom we seek are related.

Experiences create wisdom that is unchangeable.

The feeling of safety and freedom.

Journey Notes

The best city I have ever lived in is within myself, where the past gives birth to the present and future. I realize that time has changed, and even with past experiences, the future is not predictable.

Interestingly, things changed, and love became too expensive to pursue.

Everything is on the market with a different name.

Today, it's impossible not to pay for what you want.

Humanity is in the emergency room.

Success is rather how you overcome difficulties, as well as your ability to discover a new road and hidden areas in your life and not gain or achieve more.

Happiness is the condition we make for ourselves.

Give me love, hope, strength, wisdom, and peace, and I will follow you.

The Journey That I Never Planned For

The life journey that I did not plan or dream of; the civil war forced me to leave my birthplace at an early age to an unknown world. Life is a path we take; it is either predesigned for us by society, or it is something we try to design for ourselves, which is a tool we conflict with ourselves and society. What are common themes with the following words; desire, power, war, peace, soul, love, happiness, pain)? These words are too short, but they hold a powerful meaning and action. And in some ways, our life is dependent or operates on them. Believing in one, two, or all of them can have a positive or negative impact on other human life. So, the question is, who should make war and peace decisions? The answer is that there shouldn't be anyone making war or peace decisions in the first place; because promoting a violent act against another soul in itself is an immoral act. All human problems can be solved with communication. If we are all educated enough and understand life's intentions, then war should not occur in our society. The wise man does not fight or create an unsafe environment, but the fool does.

A wise man loves a debate and offers a solution, but a foolish man hates and creates an unsafe environment with violence since they have nothing to offer. My experience made me see the world differently—not the world we learn about in the classroom. Everyone is selling you something, be it a value, rules, or norms. Even the education system is engaging in the same business behavior, and it's your responsibility to identify the kind of intent. Everyone should have a clear understanding of life and the end game—the game of death and nothingness always wins; both the rich and poor will leave this earth at the end. I don't understand why there will be a second life after death when some of us never get fair treatment from God. "Or now, is it the government putting me in heaven?" I asked. The war experience created the lens through which I see darkness everywhere, and this question never leaves my mind; why is there power?

- Why are there governments?
- Where did creation take place?
- Why are there human races?

Why was slavery in Africa? What were the religious leaders' duties, morals, and roles in African slavery? Where do African weapons come from? Who provided them, and why? Is the existence of heaven true? Or is it just conceptual to a scared human?

Are hell and heaven human creations to control human behavior? If heaven exists, then the good news is that no one will enter heaven, and Jesus and his father will enjoy paradise alone forever. If a country has military forces and guns, then their chance to use the weapons to kill people is a given. Once or twice in a lifetime, some wish or hope to kill others without reason.

Think about when you were so upset and thought of ways to punish your enemy. What comes to mind first, and how do you justify it? Take five minutes and be honest with yourself; how many times in your life have you been so mad and thought of killing somebody because of political, religion, social, or race issues? Even if it's once or twice, or more, you are a danger to society, and you need help immediately.

My Journey To Khartoum

The journey to the North (Khartoum) was a five-day trip. As the war spread over the cities and villages in the South, people began to run away to neighboring towns—some even ran to nearby African countries. Others also joined the movement to fight against the Arabic colonization and religious conversion. Pariang town, which is my birthplace, is close to the North, so we walked two nights before we arrived in the city where we caught a bus to the capital. I had mixed feelings about leaving home since I didn't know where I was going and what the future held for me. The fear was about whether I would be able to go back to see my parents again or if that was the last time I'd be seeing them. My brother and I arrived in the evening. The city was not welcoming. Because of the war going on in the South, some saw us as enemies, and a good punishment for that was to be a slave, where you worked for little; but then again, there was no job. Most of the southerners did not have the skills that made them qualified to work in the workforce. Also, the language barrier was an issue; most southerners did not speak Arabic at that time. From my point of view, North Sudan was a different country; the city suffered from an identity crisis as Sudan tried so hard to be an Arab country at all costs—culturally and religiously. Sudan is in North East Africa, and historically, that is a pure African land. The word Sudan came from the black area or means dark-skinned, as they call us (read the bible). However, people confused religion with identity origination. I arrived in North Sudan at the beginning of January 1985, and I worked for a good three months as a servant, cleaning the house and floor just to survive. In mid-April of the same year, I quit. South Sudan and North Sudan separated in 2011. As of today, South Sudan is still separated from the North. Both sides made a great mistake. We should fight to the last mile in Sudan land, and Sudan will remain an African land. I believe it's the responsibility of the next generation of Africa to take Sudan back to its African motherland, and Sudan did not pay the price for what they did to the southern. Devil is among us. I do not know about you, but if you hold any ideas of hurting others because of whatever they believe or don't, then you are very much like the devil. The devil is acting as an independent object. Khartoum was better than I thought in comparison to Cairo—in terms of education. This might affect a few of them—I suspect that knowledge, in some way, takes advantage of our ignorance.

I Quit, And I Will Survive.

I arrived at Khartoum, the capital, in early 1985. There was no job for me, so one of my mother's cousins got me a job as a servant for some Arabs. I worked for three months until mid-April of that year when I quit. I moved from city to city, and each time I arrived in a city, I would start from the very bottom of society. Because of this unpleasant life journey, I have wasted more than half of my life trying to fit into societies and communities. I noticed that my identity seemed cheaper in market labor across the cities. Some still see me as was seen in the past, which means I should work for free or for very little. Society took advantage of the African conflicts that forced many citizens to leave their homes by making African citizens and immigrants cheaper labor across the world. Africa is not poor, but it seems inadequate when we compare our continent with other continents. But what we always miss in the equation is the history of the continents. The past has destroyed the very basis of humanity and identity and created a dark image of how others see Africa. The past is still reemerging in different forms. Africa might seem poor, but the problem is education. Education is the only aid needed now; a new education system is vital to reestablishing the African identity, not food. I will explain why I believe education is the key solution to African problems later in the chapter. We cannot change the past, but we can predict the future and shape it with examined ideas and visions. When I was a little boy, I believed that educated and religious people were so bright, honest, and fair and did not fight, but the war painted me an accurate picture of the world we live in. Africans in the past served as a source of income for others. African people were working for free. When others were making progress, African people were being enslaved. Where was morality or God? And today, we engage in comparison, trying to compare the African continent with other continents. When others were on the moon, Africans were running away from slavery. So how can we progress when half of the continent is still suffering mentally as a result of identity crisis, and half is still fighting for independence?

When I came to North Sudan in 1985, I did not know how to speak Arabic—I could only talk in Jieng (Dinka). I worked as a servant for three months, and in April of that year, I quit, though I did know where to go when I left. There was no alternative, but remembering my dad's farms and cattle and all the freedom I had as a child, the fact that I had to work for somebody just to survive made me angry. I said fuck life and fuck the job! Take your money and fuck yourself; I quit. You may ask, how do you leave when you don't even have a career? I refused to be poor mentally.

CHAPTER 3

MY IDENTITY, CULTURE, VALUE, AND ENEMIES

All of us showed up on earth with an empty life, no languages, culture, or religion. But associating ourselves with society, we begin to fill up our lives with family, community, society values, and norms. These tools recreate a new identity for an individual just so they could fit into a specific community. Going to North Sudan— and the fact that I was coming from a village—there were many challenges ahead of me. Some of these challenges were cultural differences and system structure that forced me to adapt to new cultures and norms that denied any identical or different culture a place in the society. And part of the challenge was that there was nothing for me anywhere, even on TV. Arabization was my new identity. In the process of adapting to a new culture and values, religious advertisement values were everywhere, and even the government was not fighting for us to maintain our identity.

They swiped out all the cultures, norms, and values that I was accustomed to since my childhood. There was nothing relative to my culture. And they succeeded in destroying me; the war in itself was a mission of culture elimination. Today, the result can be seen from the South's first generation in the North—in all aspects of dressing and naming. They never ask me what my culture can bring to the table. That's the cultural conflicts I have to pay for—and war is a cause. I am from the Jieng tribe, but my culture is no longer in me. We have different cultures and values that our morality is based on. We, the Jieng tribe, believe in God, with the exception that He lives above us. We value every life. We also believe respect is necessary; it promotes values and norms that control relationships and peace among others, and it also elevates our reputation. In terms of marriage and relationships, the Jieng tribe does not marry relatives, which was not a cause in the North. The enemy's attack bit me, and I whatever had, and it succeeded.

My Identity And Its Enemies

First off, if you were born in the city, your life is filled with different values. Second, where I came from, people (Jieng people) have unwavering values that include the Ten Commandments—not the Ten Commandments in the bible; still, it serves as the same core concept of value. The Jieng tribe has unwritten rules for everyone that must be respected and obeyed and that serves as a path for association with society. In the Jieng culture, you pay for marriage even if you do not have cows. I think Jieng does not consider a poor person; there is no free pass for the wedding without paying for the marriage.

Please look carefully at the list above and see how they influence your personal life. Everyone is selling something; each entity has its values, goals, and agendas to promote.

Society. Society's involvement in your life depends on where you are from and the society you live in. First, doctors and parents participate in your birth stages. Next, they feed you with medical and social advice, and then your parents hand you to an education system, where the damage is completed.

Did your first math teacher explain to you why one multiplied by one equals one? At the age of five, education filled and injected you with norms and values, most of which came from the world and immediately surrounded you. In addition, school sells you and your skills to businesses and the government unintentionally or intentionally, as they prepare you for the workforce—to produce goods. All of these are good, but they make you a helpful machine that operates by a set of rules.

You lost all your natural attributes. It changed the way you look at things— language and behavior wise.

Identity And Its Enemies

First, if you are born in the city, you may fill your life with different values. Second, the Jieng tribe has essential values that include ten commandments—not the Ten Commandments in the bible. Jieng has unwritten rules for everyone that must be respected and obeyed, and that serves as a center for association in the community. In the Jieng culture, you have to pay for marriage even if you do not have cows. It looks to me like Jieng does not consider a poor person; there is no free pass for the wedding without paying for marrying.

MY Identity And Its Enemies

The enemy list

- ➢ Society
- ➢ Education
- ➢ Religion
- ➢ Government
- ➢ Business

Please take a closer look at the list above and see how it influences your personal life. Everyone is selling something; each entity has its values, goals, and agendas to promote.

Society.

Society's involvement in your life depends on where you are from and the society you live in. First, doctors and parents participate in your birth process. Next, they feed you with medical and social advice, and then your parents hand you to an education system, where the damage is completed.

Did your first math teacher explain to you why one multiplied one equals one? At the age of five, education filled and injected you with norms and values, most of which came from the world and immediately surrounded you. In addition, school sells you and your skills to businesses and governments unintentionally or intentionally, as they prepare you for the workforce—to produce goods. All of these are good, but they make you a helpful machine that operates by a set of rules.

You lost all your natural attributes. It changed the way you look at things—language and behavior wise.

Let us take Deng as an example. Deng went to school at age five and graduated from high school at 18 and college at 23. He got a job at a local bank and got married at age 27. He had three children and retired from the bank after 50 years.

What language does Deng speak now at the age of 72?

The business sends you to the end of your life, just like a bus stop—and this is how we lost our identity, respectfully. So, on the promise of happiness, always remember that there will always be one winner in every game held, and that is no different from working in a business environment—you are given little to survive.

YOU lost every attribute. Therefore, the goals you achieve through another are not yours.

No Answer Questions

Before entering into the 'no answer questions' of life

With Deng as an example

Are you in a pure state? Pure as an independent unit that can live without being mixed with other elements of influence? A person born in a village is like a city-born person, but he or she might have a different effect on him/her (individuality and identity purity)—if it even exists. Enemies of identity or oneself (pure as a single unit that has not been mixed with anything else cannot be found in this life), and that's what bothers me more than anything else. I later discovered that I am not me. Therefore, my question is, how much is purely me without the influence of others? In addition, my concern is that my identity and culture have been destroyed by society, religion, government, business, and education systems. They control my consciousness and my daily decisions on acting and behaving in public and in private. Two of the concepts or words that I hate most are "in the beginning," which is found in the Bible, and "human freedom is a unique entity."

Humans cannot be completely free from the influence of others. The freedom of individuals from society's influence is impossible. Human is not accessible because it is a social animal. Their lives are connected to other animals. Another part of our individuality or ourselves as a unique person is controlled or taken by society.

- Because it is a social animal—its living is connected to other animals.
- Individuality and freedom are a percentage (%).
- Another part of our person is controlled or taken by society.
- Does individuality even exist?
  - Pure – oneself – as an independent entity does not exist.
  - Existing oneself and survival seems impossible
- Factors and elements that cause Association – related – belonging – to be related
  - Needs

- Acceptance seeking
- We can
- Resistance
- Rebel
- To live or to be

➤ How can you survive in an ocean of human beings?
- It seems impossible to eliminate society's influence on an individual's life.

➤ How can you be an independent entity, even with the influence of an outsider?
- World—Can you choose not to be a part of society?
- Humans have many capabilities, and one of them is the ability to become anything we want to be. Prepare By society.
- People influence each other's actions or behavior in partial or whole, creating public and private behaviors.

CHAPTER 4

A PEACEFUL CITY FOR ALL

―――――― ❧❦❧ ――――――

The city is for us all.
We are all equal in human attributes.
We can be happy together.
We can share the earth peacefully; it is a roof for all of us.

We all deserve to live in peace. A peaceful city is associated with a peaceful society that is well organized, where everyone deserves to live, and where everyone contributes equally with ideas that benefit the wellbeing of the people. The city is for all of us, not just you, but us. It is where the individual or group contribution benefits all within the society or community. This city can be created if each individual has a great understanding of the value of humans and humanity through awareness and education, not just beliefs. That city of wise societies where everyone deserves to live should be a global roof for us all. The city that I, you, and we have in mind is that in which we all share the earth equally and have the same rights. The morality of war and those Soldiers sent to the war have nothing to do with the war itself; they are victims like anyone else. We should not send any person to fight until they have high education and well-examined morals and motives. This standard should include the leaders in charge of war decision-making. **We should not send any person to war and least he or she has a high education and well examined morally and motivate intend that included the leader who are in charge of war decision making.** Electing incompetent individuals will always result in unintended outcomes. Peace, joy, and happiness bring out the best in humanity, which is what we want—to be happy and safe here on earth. The earth is a city where the people live in peace, and all the citizens have equal human rights. For everyone to live happily and safely, it is the responsibility of each individual to act accordingly in order to maintain peace among themselves. Keep in mind that the achievement of a peaceful city requires the entire city to be willing to live in peace. As you can see around the world today, war is the language of resolving conflicts. The language of war is an indication of hate and incapability to solve disagreement, and we should know that, in every war, souls will be lost forever. I lost three of my brothers and parents. They died in the Sudan civil war when I was in the North. The unbalanced power between the nations is still a major cause of the wars we see today. North Korea and the United States cannot go to war easily because of the weapons that each country has. War is a business; everyone is selling something to the other side, be it the government or weapons makers. If we want to stop the war going on around the world, we first have to cease weapons manufacturing. This may be complicated since these companies also want to profit and pay bills at the end of the week. The discontinuation of the weapons manufacturing debate is hard to win, but it can be achieved if intended. Temporal and partial peace can be achieved if there's a collective effort of the citizens. Peace should be a goal for the stability of each city or nation in the world.

- Can we achieve it?
- What is the challenge?
- Do we need peace, and why?

Peace is a term or word that has no significant meaning until the peaceful mind uses it with intent.

Let's assume for a moment that God exists.

All agreed

And the questions become; does He have an eye, physical body, soul, emotion? Where does He live? And does He control the earth and human behavior, including desire?

If all assumptions above are true;

- Where do these happenings in the world today come from?
- Why was evil created in the first place?
- I'm bothered greatly by the existence of a good God that allows killing and death.

Let us assume for a moment and say that all living things on earth are self-made from the reaction and interconnections of two or more objects (for example, male and female intercourse). As a result, the connected parts create an independent object, for example, children. Treat human aging as a separation of the connected parts from one another based on their attributes, and that's what we call 'death.' Because death can be considered the end-of-life cycle of the soul and the physical components, even a healthy person will reach a certain stage where their physical components cannot move. The physical component of living things carries the soul. The interconnection of both creates a second independent object that can be seen as a different object, linked to the original image of the first part self-made (parents and children). Some of the self-made provided a great power that created a soul, physical body, and life, and the soul is not centrally governed; instead, all are independent in factions.

Let's assume for a moment that God is powerful, loving, and has eyes as well.

- ➤ Questions may immediately arise;
- ➤ What does He look like?
- ➤ Where does He live?
- ➤ Can He see?

Countless crimes are being committed worldwide against humanity, even at this moment; this leaves no room to believe there's an existing greatest, kind, powerful creature that has eyes and ears. The world, including living things in danger, lets you wonder how happiness, peace, and safety can be achieved in this dangerous city. A city where human souls are lost every day—some are killed without second thought, and where people have no respect for their fellow humans. Slaves, race, or class are destroyed without regret at all. With all these happenings, we've seen that life is in motion toward death. Whether you are happy or safe, young or old, we will all get to the end-of-life cycle. The life of any man at the end is equal to zero; life is like an object that goes up with a negative number and comes down with a positive number to the same point where it started before going up. We live life, whether long or short, on earth at the end; life and death cancel one another out. The same idea applies to living things being born and dying; no matter how long you live, in the end, the physical components and the soul expires. That is even and fair to all humans; it doesn't differentiate between one who lives longer or shorter, one who is happy or sad, rich or poor, boy or girl, or even race—death wins all the time. You will not experience your own death, so take life easy and do what you think interests you—it is a stupid journey.

The Love
War, Peace, Love, And Happiness. What Are The Common Themes Of These Concepts In Human Life?

Let me share my thoughts about love because it is the father of all things, which brings about life and happiness. Love is a topic I wanted to write about when I was in college, but I was a computer major, so it was not relevant to my field of study. However, I will write about this in the chapter as part of my life experiences.

How Did It Come About?

When I was in college, I went on a date with a lady. We met outside the mall parking lot before we went to the restaurant.

As soon as I got out of my car, she said, "You have a very nice car."

These words never left my mind; in my defense, she loves my car more than me. Can't she be nice and say something about me since this was our first time meeting in person, before describing my car? And what you have to know about me is, I am a 'why,' 'how,' and 'what' kind of person; therefore, I have become curious about love. I thought many times in college to write about it, but I did not, and now it's time to share it with you. I will assume that you have been in love or you are in love right now. Either way, I want you to take a deep look inside your heart to discover why you love who you love. With or without awareness, you find yourself fulfilling inner needs, wants, desires, and expectations in many cases.

Elements Of Love

Million reasons to fall in Love

I am Wur Deng, a secret love explorer, and I will be your guide throughout this video to rediscover the Love secret.

Anything we want or need falls into three of these elements;

- ➢ Desiring
- ➢ Fulfillment
- ➢ Expectation.

I am here to help you get the answer you need and deserve from your partner, and it's a clear, specific intellect. Always remember that you live once on earth; therefore, it is wise to not waste time with people who bring no value into your life. Most of us know that every day is a love day/month, and when we are too busy, we forget what to say or what gift to buy to express our gratitude and appreciation of love. As life goes on, some of us will fail to fulfill love elements in terms of words or actions.

But not to worry, I am here to provide you with a suggestion to help you create questions that will generate answers. Be specific, and avoid the general questions that produce unwanted responses. Your question can go like this; what is the thing you love or like about me the most?

What are the five things you love about me? What are things you believe I need to do to improve our relationship? When he or she fails to answer correctly, that is a red flag. Sometimes, we make mistakes in expressing our feeling; and throughout history, the wrong question (how much do you love me?) has been asked so many times. First of all, love is uncountable and cannot be measured because it is emotional energy triggered by desire and expectations; also, the word Love is countless.

You may ask, how did you discover the secret of Love? The bible gave me the answer. In the bible, the condition is given to the first human by God to obey him, for judgment is death. Love is no different. We give love to get a reward. Today, heaven is still under the same condition; God says follow my commitments and laws, or your judgment in the end time is hell. My purpose is to make you reassess your assumption about love. So first, in your word, what is love?

Define love without looking it up in the dictionary, then compare your answers.

Why do we have to reassure people we love every day?

Can we measure love? And if so, what is the unit of love?

Love is a word and an action in its intent, depending on what you take toward the lover.

Love is a word that does not mean anything until it is shown with progressive action.

We know from grammar class that that word means nothing.

Love is a choice we make in every moment that passes.

The wrong question has always been asked: how much do you love me?

Love is either association, sharing, alignment, fulfilling, or expectations.

Keep in mind that the degree of love strength and emotions depends on many factors.

The following are a few on the list that play a role in love and emotions.

Values that a person holds

- Norms
- Society
- Region
- Education
- Religion

- Beliefs
- Race
- Awareness

Knowing what you want in life and having a clear understanding of the elements of love can save you time and money and also keep you away from divorce court.

What are the common themes of these concepts in human life?

- Love
- Happiness.
- War
- Peace

So, What Are Love Ingredients?

Love ingredients or components are associated with things we love and may seem obvious. But not to worry, I will break it down for you. Love is a word that means nothing until it is put into action; it is a choice we make in every moment that passes. Let's take marriage as an example. If you ask a married couple why they got married, you might find a million different answers, and the simple answer is that each person is filling a void of different needs, wants, and expectations to satisfy their missing inner desires. If this expectation is not satisfied or met, the love becomes less effective. Love's supportive elements have to be kept alive for the love to continue. The practices are a magic key for love to succeed. Have you ever watched a food show where professional food tasters judge chefs?

You may be wondering how they differentiate the tastes of many foods, while ordinary people may notice just the sweet or salty flavor.

The wrong question has been asked: how much do you love me?

What Does Love Mean?

Love is simply an association, desire, want, sharing, alignment, and fulfilling expectations.

Love is the emotional energy that creates the power that enables you to fulfill each other's needs. And when you establish a channel of love, it flows bidirectional, connecting and associating you with others, whether you are the sender or receiver. Disappointment arises when you fail to meet their expectations or fulfill their desires or needs. So, what is the root of love that makes an individual associate with and gives love or energy to others?

The right question can be like this; what is the one thing you love /like about me the most?

What are the things you love about me?

What are things you believe I need to work on to strengthen our relationship?

Sometimes, we mistakenly express our love in the wrong way, and that produces an emotionally undesirable result. How much do you love? I do not know. Can you measure love? If so, what is the unit of love?

Why Should I Love You?

This question is not a philosophical question; instead, it intends to determine what values you can add or bring into your love life; and the answer depends on what I have mentioned above. So next time you meet someone, please ask the right questions to generate the correct answers. Most of us are aware that every day is a love day. Valentine's Day came and went. We were busy thinking about what to gift, expressing gratitude, and some failed to find suitable words of expression. So, at this moment, what are the love choices you're about to make?

Happiness zone

Your happiness resides in the love department within you; it is not how much but how you choose to live. Interestingly, when you learn how to be your own happiness creator, you become unstoppable. That is the difference between unhappy and happy individuals, and it comes down to the wisdom of not seeking happiness outside of your control area zone.

How do you want to be seen outside the world and inside of your world?

How do you want others (including close relatives and loved ones) to see you? We live in two worlds (private and public) in one body, but we want the public to see a different picture of us. Life created another image that puts oneself in conflict mode because we want to be received differently in school, work, and in relationships. Matching two worlds is the key to a successful and happy life, and this matching can be accomplished by fulfilling the needs and how you want to be seen.

Do You Feel The Outside World Misunderstood You?

And what areas in your life does the outside world misunderstand?

Having straightforward questions can assist you in reassessing and realigning your life.

If we do not have a solid foundation, the outside world can take over and control our life. The first question you should ask yourself is, what do you want to be? Having an image in your heart becomes a matter of how to get there; it's like knowing where you are going.

War, peace, love, and happiness are human creations. Therefore, you have to be an independent thinker because the power is within you. You are a god in your terms; never waste any moment because a clock never stops to wait for your conditions to be right. Find your love ingredients. We all have been in love. Loving something or someone occurs when elements that cause someone to fall in love exist, and when we are unsure, we create experiences and unsatisfied situations that lead to less love and happiness. When serving in a restaurant, we don't know all ingredients in the food, but one taste can be satisfying. It's the same as falling in love; we fall in love without knowing why we love others, and that can be troubling.

My Purpose

My purpose is to make you reassess your assumption about love.

Why do we have to reassure people we love every day?

So first, in your own words, what is love?

Define love without looking at the meaning in the dictionary, then compare your answers.

Can we measure love? And if so, what is the unit of love?

Love is a word and, at the same time, an action—depending on what you take toward the lover.

One thing for sure is that you don't fully replace the love source in you.

You've realized by now that I am not giving you an answer. Instead, I'm giving you the questions. The reason is that love depends on many things and factors such as society's values, beliefs, religions, awareness, education, and so on. Therefore, it is hard to give one answer. But I can provide general, root, source, and education to help think critically. Just like religions intend to align their actions to God's calling, you base your love on values. Values are predefined rules that govern your inner behavior. Remember that each individual has two behaviors, public and private, and those who take their private behavior to the public can be seen as weird because they cannot control their private lives.

Love is about fulfilling promises and desires.

Meet the society standard and get married.

But the question is, to who?

Ask your inside world about love.

What do you not love about yourself?

At least, there is one thing you don't like about yourself"?

And this is the beginning of my discussion.

We get married for many reasons, and for whatever reason, you should be clear on that.

Your desire and clarity will assist and direct to right and lease fixing

What are the values that a loving container should contain?

We lie to ourselves that we love someone so much and complete the lie with "I know it."

We only want or need what others possess (contain)—can be whatever you desire, enjoy, or need—so we start associating and aligning with them in order to meet and satisfy our wants and desires; in other words, love is a medium that carries out love. Love generates and creates an emotional frequency in various degrees and becomes a center where the two lovers meet. For instance, a sighted person may have a different experience than a blind individual—a sighting person has different views. Love can be created and repaired in the light of emotional intellect by assessing wants.

The Untold Truth About Love

Our lives depend partly on wanting, desiring, and pursuing things within wherein value is received. And love is the magic word that breaks the ice

Senseless free when it comes to love

Love is an expectation-driven motion that generates enough frequency power within desire and courage in the form of action. One thing is certain, half of the feelings we call love is an unexamined assumption about another receiving end. And the whole sense comes down to expectation value—production result.

CHAPTER 5

THOSE WHO DIE ON THE FRONT LINE AND BEHIND THE WAR

Each war battle has a front line, and Sudan's civil war's front line was in the Southern part of the country. On the battlefield where our heroes fought, some were killed on the front line so we could have freedom. After the war, millions of people (children and the elderly) and animals died from a lack of food. Meanwhile, Khartoum, Sudan's capital, was a slow death place, where many people died because the city had nothing to offer. People who came from the South did not have the skills, hence, joining the workforce. People were living in displaced camps, also known as "refugee camps," surrounding the capital. 'Refugees' is the name given to those who run away from war.

The South and the North were two different countries in terms of language and religious beliefs. People in North Sudan speak Arabic, while most people in the South speak a local African language or English. Sudan was divided even before the actual separation on July 9, 2011. These challenges disqualify the Southerners from joining the workforce in the North.

Also, most places were not accepting Southerners to work because of religious laws; most businesses are owned by Muslim believers and do not allow Christians to lead their companies or organizations. Some people could not even try to find a job, and these camps were open prisons of death because the environment was hot and not healthy for living. The only option for some young people was to sell water on the streets. -another job was selling water to residents that carried it on the back of a donkey and its two barrels joined, and each barrel held 6 gallons of water; these were the means of living. Another type of job was shoes shining in the streets. Some people were homeless. People could not afford to go to the hospital or school. As people experience these difficulties, Sudan saw the world through one lens—religion and what you believe in. Unbelievers are evil in their views and ways and have no values, now or Day of Judgment. Believing in God was the only way to survive in North Sudan, and if you did not believe in God, you had to fake it. And those who do not believe in God considered being evil and losers. We were refugees in our own country and land. Religion caused Sudan's division, and that remained a dark place in North East Africa forever. Today, if you want to rent a hotel with your wife, you are required to have a marriage certificate to enter the hotel. In 1989, after the Islamic government came to power on June 30, things changed to

360 degrees—it became a worse time in Sudan's history. Sudan became two broken parts where people lived in two parallel worlds—believers and unbelievers. Unbelievers are enemies of the country, and they'll be punished in hell at the end of the world on the Day of Judgment. South Sudan lives in a dangerous neighborhood that sees the world as a one-way street in all the dark times. The war was in the past, but memories and impact were carried on, and these are not opinions but facts and experiences. South Sudan's crisis had a political structure that limited the South's development, even before Sudan's independence in 1956. Inequality forced the South to go to war with the North.

When people face unfairness, limited options of peace and freedom become less available, and violence and war become unavoidable. South Sudanese had no choice but to engage themselves in the war that destroyed everything, including values, cultures, and national identities. The South asked for equality in political opportunities and resource distribution by the laws; the Christians and Blacks could not lead any position and could be only vice president or vice-chair. You would expect the God-fearing people to do the right thing, including treating others human regardless of their beliefs, but surprisingly, that was not the case in Sudan civil war.

The war left nothing but death behind. Ask tough questions that may not have actual or satisfactory answers. Some of these are whether God exists and how you know He is responding to your prayers. At the same time, it is not straightforward to deny or accept that the beautiful world accidentally appeared without intent or was designed by an intelligent mind. My question is always not about if God exists. Instead, about God's nature, undoubtedly, the existing powerful, brilliant mind created all things, including me. He might not know about the future—the story of Adam and Eve might make you assume that the creator lacks knowledge of future events. Another way is to look at all existing things and their interaction that could result in different physical objects. The sin of Adam and Eve, which caused the death, lets you assume you have a six-month-baby in the middle of the room, and there is a deep hole close to the table, and on the table is the milk. You know that if you leave your child alone in the room, he/she will go for the milk. However, for some reason, when leaving the room, you decide to put a sign that reads "do not go to the table, and if you do, you will fall in the hole," knowing very well that your baby cannot read. Adam did not know the meaning of death, even if God told them not to eat from a tree. The idea that claims death came from sin does not meet the rational thinking by all accounts—it is cheap to sell. Likewise, it is not effortless to be contained in a controlled guide by a sensible object. Let us first assume these three possibilities exist but have no soul, making Him unresponsive or unreachable to world events. Maybe the aim of living a simple life is nothing more than just a temporary event, which has nothing to do with creation. The third and final possibility is that life is an interaction of two different objects that reacts to an imbalance in quantity and quality. For example, to make a baby, you need two different genders—to create other independent living things. And as necessary to share, it aims to benefit the next generation. Why are Black children called Black even when they have mixed race parents? **Wherever may be and take away is why were black people, not other races?** The future is occurring. Who is a friend or enemy? You have to be mindful, and the reason is that I am not an expert on any topic of religion. Still, my contact with those who hold different opinions than me as a believer advises that these experiences are eligible for debate and that static and dynamic thinking is needed to move forward. Our values and beliefs should not be a wall standing between us; humanity is enough to bind us together.

CHAPTER 6

I WISH GOD COULD CHANGE THE CIRCUMSTANCES.

When crises or any life situation occurs that overpowers your ability, you are forced to ask for help, and most often, we wish that God could change the circumstances. In most cases, we use power to prevent the event from happening and pray to God. But not knowing if God is listening to the prayer creates unpleasant feelings. Asking for help from God was the only option we had because the government that was supposed to protect us was the one doing the killing. God's silence sometimes makes you have a hard time believing in the existence of the powerful creator. A creator that is unresponsive to human suffering or unwilling to punish those who do wrong to other human beings. Life is not easy to ride; it is complex and challenging, and facts and truth are decentralized, meaning there is no source of truth where we retrieve the world's facts. For that reason, it is difficult for individuals or groups to claim knowledge of anything that is purely truthful, whether it is religious beliefs. Life is complicated; some get it, and some don't. Some work hard to figure out what makes sense and is meaningful. Others offer their reasoning and explanation. Have you ever asked questions about the purpose of life and what we gain from living on earth? Really, what do we do again in life? If you ask people with different backgrounds, you will get different answers based on their beliefs, education level, and age.

Let me give simple exercises; ask a married couple why they got married. You might hear what you did not expect to hear, but it is true. Each one of us holds a different interest, and in return, we have a different need, and that dictates our decision-making, awareness, ignorance, and expectation. "In the beginning" is a phrase (which is found in the Bible - Old Testament) that tells us that there was a beginning, and the question becomes; what was before the beginning? What was before the creation of the world we live in today? None for sure can give you pure/clear evidence without referencing the same book written by the first human writers, *"Why God created the world."* Is there a purpose for human existence? If so, to do what to who? Is backward thinking a necessity for human existence? Do not bother to search for truth, and the reason is that the life/death of humans traces back to the purpose of the first humans. Without death, all these seem like evidence. All were here in power until separation happened, making some more valuable than others. The idea of the "beginning" makes you ask yourself endless questions. For example, if there was a beginning, what was before the start? Do you realize that human beings do nothing for God in all time we spend on earth? Revisit religious prayers and see if you can come across the phrase "God help God"; is all we do in life for human interest and welfare? We never understood why animals also die if human death is a result of the crime committed by the first parents. You never study when you are about to take an exam—and you are expecting to pass the exam?

With God, how you would have suffered—from God's goodness—one thing for sure is that the creator has the power to make. But in free fall, our fear projects and produces an imagined independent power; life is a weak part of the energy with a timestamp. The living could be in an endless existence. The life of living things might not hold meaningful value. As we perceive the ideas of existing, "forever" may not originate from existing. Therefore, suffering and struggles may not be the center of the purposes and thoughtfulness of creation. **We think we know little of the sense that fulfills living to live the life you human confidence in time and energy.** Move we advance in life living interference our reality thinking -non-independent -fear - the result -Other or. What are the ten key messages of my book?

Why Do We Fear Death When None Cares?

Life is like a dead road; whether it is long or short, it leads nowhere; it is a zero result of self-unawareness. Soon, the soul and the physical body will be separated. Then you hit the end of no return. So why do we fear death, especially when no one cares about us and our existence as humans? Interestingly, when death occurs, we cannot describe our life experience afterlife separation. It is similar to the light switch (on/off) where you cannot tell if the light was on or off on moment action desire. If you enter a dark room, you will not know whether the light was on before joining the room. This is similar to our soul's departure; others will have bad experiences with your departure, but you are gone forever, so why is death so scary.

When the war broke out, humans and animals died; and another problem was that there was no running water in the houses. Water pump machines in Pariang town were being used by soldiers, so they were not accessible at that time. The villages surrounding the city depended on the rainy season. Because of war, people could not travel to water sources. It usually takes three to four months before we would get water. We couldn't defend or fight the enemy; their forces were more powerful than ours. The real question was, why were they killing us? We did not know who to ask for help. When you are helpless and powerless, you no longer fear death because your life is in the hands of the enemy. It was hard to watch the animals dying from lack of water and food. It was a scary time, especially not knowing what the enemy was thinking, and we had nothing to defend ourselves. It was the darkest time. South Sudan had suffered enough, and we needed God to intervene immediately. When the willingness to live is more significant to a young person who wants to explore the world, threats and death are useless. The will to live created fears, especially when there wasn't any reason not to die and God was nowhere. Challenges were so crucial to be handled by humans; we didn't have the ability to protect our own lives from danger on all accounts. God was not responsive. Millions of people died in the Sudan civil war, and both God and the rest of the world were in deep silence or turned away from us. The battle partly has religious aspects, which is exposing and forcing the people to accept the religion. The goal was to make South Sudan a spiritual gateway to Africa for the introduction to Arabicization. Responding to our necessity, it was a time I wanted to live with my lovely parents and brothers, but God was nowhere to be found. In early 1984, the Sudan-Arabic government attacked the cities and villages in South Sudan.

The unbalancing war in power and help from God was a need, especially since there were no weapons to face the enemy. The question always arises; what part of human life does God protect or concern Himself with? The safety of the human soul should be the core center of God's existence, especially when death comes with unwillingness. Unbalancing power between the North and the South was notable. The world and God were far away to offer help to the people of South Sudan. I learned and experienced from the war that life experiences are simply about the fact that we are black. Others think we do not deserve to live or even have human rights. With that mindset, society and the city that we hope for cannot now or forever be achieved. Others still have different agendas toward other human beings. My war experiences left me with non-answer questions, or no one was simply interested in giving the correct answers. Growing up in Sudan, I can say Africa will remain a third world for a very long time until they change their imagination and the way they see the world. Religions: So many African churches and Muslim places of worship, and still, the continent has a high poverty rate. Africans have been drugged with ideas that do not exist. Africans pray more than other continents do. Apparently, Africans have been told that God is a solution; pray for five to six hours, and God will send food to you.

You pray for five hours? What? Do you think God is deaf? Africa needs to turn on an emergency light for 200 years without religion to improve the human condition on the continent. Let's assume that God exists, and one thing for sure is that He does not hand out gifts overnight. The reason is that He created everything you need to survive and made everything equally available for all from the beginning of creation; to have it, all you need to do is to use your sense. Even if you go to the moon to cry to God, it is pointless. We see in physical form that our lives result from imagination, and those who focus more on vision know the product in light. Hence, your world is given to you by the power of your dream, no more or less. What do you eat when you grow? Famine in Africa is still a problem when it should not be because everything is available, the land—no more asking from God. What is not available are leaders and imagination. People are led by outdated thinkers who are so behind and not even qualified to be bus drivers. Right now, what we ask our kids is, what do they want to be when they grow up? But the question should be, what do you eat when you grow up? Teach them to go to the moon without getting help from others. The answer is the day when the people will have absolute independence with their imaginations.

Most Africans depend on outside aides; it is a result of their inability to think and produce from what they have. First, Africa needs to take a look at the education system in the world today. Presently, kids still depend on teachers as sources of information; they are not teaching them to think by themselves. They teach western history and scientific discoveries from the west, and that impacts how they view their own countries. We should teach children greatness, some from God, and some from other humans. For your existence, everything, including languages, existed before you. The one who created the earth made everything available for you, so it is up to you to go get it. I was born in the South Sudan region, which later became the Republic of South Sudan. The South was part of Sudan until 2011, when it split from Sudan after the prolonged civil war from 1956-1972 and 1983-2005. It then got trapped in another war, and things got worse. Life is a dead road that leads nowhere. We are in a continuous loop, thinking we are making progress, but it reverses in nature. Soon, it is a moment of birth, and then the age count back to zero; whether the life is long or short, it will produce no result that ends in self-unawareness. Think of life as having a lot of money and then losing all of them.

Dialogue Between Deng And Lueth About The Nature Of God

Nature of God

Mr. Deng: How far are you from the truth?

Mr. Lueth: What truth?

Mr. Deng: The truth about God: that He controls the entire creation affair—is it an oversight?

Mr. Lueth: Don't you think? The question should be, what is the nature of God? And I dislike the phrase (in the beginning). If the world has a starting point, what was before that? And you cannot say "there was nothing before."

Mr. Deng: I do know that God is powerful and peaceful.

Mr. Lueth: Let me stop you right there. How would you explain the suffering, killing, and unfairness, injustices in the world? If He is powerful, why does He allow these things to happen?

Mr. Deng: These suffering, killing, and injustice have nothing to do with God. These are purely human acts.

Mr. Lueth: So then tell me, what part of human life is God interested in or concerned with?

Mr. Deng: God gives life, food, air, and all other necessities to live.

Mr. Lueth: The things you are telling me already exist; they interact and produce a similar part (object), which links back to the origin. Let's say your mother and father because of two identical in origin but have different attributes?

Mr. Deng: I'm not sure that I follow. Are you suggesting that life is the result of different parts interacting?

Mr. Lueth: That is what evidence suggests, and you cannot give me one reason why animals die when they've not committed any crime against God; that is the definition of unfairness.

Mr. Deng: I think you lost sense because of what you called suffering. You always have choices in any life event, and death, in God's eye, means a different thing; because instead, you are going to another world where you will be judged for what you did on earth (world).

Mr. Lueth: How do I know what choice to make when the world is full of evil? And don't you think it is God's duty to control all evil deeds?

Mr. Deng: God gives you a free choice, and you have to choose what suits your lifestyle.

Mr. Lueth: Based on what you said, I want peace, safety, and a peaceful world where we all live equally.

Mr. Deng: What I can tell you is that you are living in peace right away. Pain and suffering are soul nature, but you can create your own perfect and peaceful world in your image. Do you know there is nothing like 'enemy' or 'friend'? But you have chosen them based on your own belief. Remember that war and peace are human's creations; it has nothing to do with God.

Mr. Lueth: So then, what is God's role in human life?

I want to see God take control over what humans cannot control or desire.

Let us continue.

The end.

Day will come.

The day will come, and you realize I am not your enemy.

One day you will learn the language of beauty and the language of love.

One day the Sun of freedom will shine on us all.

Let us live together.

Let us love one another.

We are all result of the power that creates and provides a soul equally.

We are all products of our parents, whether we intended or accidentally found ourselves in an unexplanatory event. There are a million reasons to get married and a million reasons the man and the woman have sex. Imagine you were there the night the two (parents) started conversing, then decided to continue the conversation outside and later walked back inside. Things felt right, and then it turned physical—complete that thought. We all have a past event; whether you were born before or after marriage, there's no reason for someone to kill you.

CHAPTER 7

I WAS BORN BLACK AND BECAME BLACK BY SOCIETY'S DEFINITION

Being a human was no man's idea. Instead, it was someone else's idea—the power that everything is rooted in; therefore, to that power, I will obey. Moreover, being black was intended by the power that governs the living, so I will not go to court with those who disvalue me.

If you are old enough, you come to realize that society's lifestyle choices influence your life and how to live, even without direct involvement. From career to education-wise, it is vital for the community to give its members a sense of belonging and inclusion even without direct involvement. Each one of us plays a different role in society. Consideration, equal opportunity, and belonging as a respectful member of that society or community are critical factors for involvement and building a solid culture. Lack of equal opportunity created unbalanced living status, values, culture, and power.

From my experiences, Blackness is more than a skin color—it is a container in which they put anything that's related to your Blackness without a second thought about your ability as a human being. And the history of slavery added more to it, making it a belief of others that whatever related to your Blackness is black. My experiences gave me evidence that society has already made up its mind that black is invaluable. Can you feel it in your bone in the education system, workforce, and social classes order? Do you ever wonder who gives a human being the right to kill and eat an animal? Black people were killed and treated like animals. We know that animals do not sin—as the bible claims—but humans do sin, so why do we kill chickens, cows, and other animals? It is no different from the way others see and treat black people. We are not valuable enough in the eyes of others, even in our own land of Africa. Even the change that seems to be happening is suitable for only conferences and elections; there should not be a South Sudan but one country, Sudan. There is only one choice, either those who call themselves Arabs live with Africans, respectfully the landowners, or go back to where they came from, period.

From East To West As I Moved From City To City.

My parents did not teach me about the world and my skin color; I am less of a human being or less intelligent than other races. I was born, and grew up in a small town, then moved to the capital. My first interaction with other races was in the Pariang town church. Nevertheless, there was not much talk about color. Church members were referred to as fathers and sisters until I left the city. My last Christmas at the church was 12/25/1984. With that short time experiences, I can confidently say that we Africans are peaceful human beings. There was no incident against these church members, and I never heard anyone being racist. I came to North Sudan at the beginning of 1985, and that was where I came to experience my Blackness. I was not qualified for anything, even with my level of education. I had to hide my books during my studies in primary and middle school, as well as my first time in college, Sudan University of Science and Technology.

Still, I had no value in others' eyes. I was working as a tea/coffee boy for non-graduate individuals. It is a system designed to serve only those who designed it; they control the rules, laws, media, and system, and everyone is scared to disagree with it. Egypt was the worst of all. In Egypt, they called you by your skin color (/chocolate/brown) or asked you to give them time to look at your skin. These are cities you would expect to know better. My worst experience was when I was in a rural area, I stopped at a small shop to get something to eat, and the children surrounded me. This left me wondering if these children have ever watched sports or movies on TV where many black people play. I had many experiences in colleges in America as well; you would hear questions you are not expecting from a college student about Africa—it's sad on every level. Educate yourself if you want to learn more about others, or shut the fuck up. Even at this moment, I sometimes get this question; we do education background and background checks. Is there something we should know?

My College Experiences

A short story during my community college years, sometime in 2007 or 2008—I was at the financial office to check my financial aid. The process was: You sign up at the front desk, and then you take a seat at the waiting area. About 20 to 25 students were waiting. It got to my turn, and a lady came out. She stood there pointing at me, so I asked her if she was referring to me, and she acknowledged, so I followed her, laughing the whole time; how did she figure out it was me? There was nothing wrong with that, but it gave me a sense of what happens during job recruiting. Whenever I send my resume to the recruiting manager, she/he can quickly identify me by name. I experienced all of that, so I decided to put my picture on my email account after many interviews. Even with a master's degree in Computer Information and Network Security, I cannot find a job.

Blackness is not just the skin and its social status; it's the human class container in which anything that's related to black skin is dropped in, regardless of your background. There is still society's conscious refusal to acknowledge black people's ability in terms of the races' contribution to the well-being of society and humanity. The lack of employment opportunities and education has an impact on lifestyle and values. Look at Africa's leaders in the United Nations— none were able to make their speeches. Why? I do not know, but you can figure that out— without saying anything, your action says a lot.

Let me start with religious (Christian) teachings in Africa—the devil's color is black. I used to practice the Catholic religion when I was growing up in South Sudan, and the church used to show us movies/films where the devil was black; this leaves a negative view of the color black, in general. Additionally, all the children with mixed race parents, in the end, are labelled Black. It's society's rejection of black people and their skin or whatever is associated with their Blackness. These practices cannot be viewed differently from the belief that black people are less intelligent. However, I couldn't be prouder of the Black leaders, actors, musicians, and sports players of the past, as well as the present, who have demonstrated that they are gifts of the creator.

CHAPTER 8

LONG-SUFFERING, AND NO ENDING SOON.

Those who fear being in peace with others are the enemies of peace.

Jesus was here on earth a thousand years ago.

And his message was a sense of peace, forgiveness, and life after death. Yet today, the world is more dangerous than before. Just the push of a few buttons could wipe out every life on earth. People become smartest and more confident as they advance, which raises the question of God's existence as an entity that governs and oversees all things existing. With the current complications of things on the planet, the question of the presence of a God could not serve the assumption or room for the logic and intellect argument of reality itself. Instead, the fair question could be, what is the nature of God? And the simple answer is that God is how you want it to be for you. Your belief is a god. God is not an independent entity but the energy that your belief and desire activate.

South Sudan

The long coming freedom and celebration did not last long before entering a new war.

The civil war between the North and South Sudan ended in 2005. That peace allowed the South to gain independence in 2011. In 2013, two years after, war broke out in the new country; why? My older brother went back to South Sudan after independence, and he was forced to join the army without training. As a result, he was killed in July 2017. The War between South and North Sudan was for the cost of freedom that ended the Arabic inhabitation in the South. The second war of the South was a lack of leadership and vision. Many people remained in North Sudan, and others lived in refugee camps in neighboring countries. Almost two generations were born in North Sudan and other countries; they've never been to the South. Fear and disappointment are the greatest. Sudan conflicts have been around for so long; even before the one that broke out in 1983, there was a civil war between the south and north.

South Sudanese suffered long enough, and many lives were lost in conflict.

With the conflicts in South Sudan, the problem is more profound than one issue. The country is in survivor mode, and God knows when to get us out of it. There is no single solution or diagnosis to South Sudan's problem.

To make sense of and address these conflict topics, we have to be honest when assessing the issues. Upfront, know that I am not a social researcher, but I will point you to some of the factors worth examining.

My assumption began to point to those factors. As we try to find the answers to failure and misgovernance, a few factors come to mind: the following are some of the factors;

- War impact
- Education system
- Environment
- Belief

The country has military rules mindset; many feel there is one who liberates the country.

- Lack of accountability
- Lack of standard procedures for appointing or electing leaders within the South Sudan government.

The factors listed above have impacts and contribute to individual behavior and the way they look at things.

Let us begin with the population of South Sudan, a basic understanding of governance, and then the relationship between citizens and leaders—the awareness gap is wide.

Most of the population, including today's leaders, were refugees in Khartoum. Nothing could come out of there or be expected of the leaders because some were servants and had no experience or confidence to lead the nation. Some of them have never had a regular job. Therefore, we should not be surprised by the country's failure. I suggest that people create a new vision for South Sudan's future in order to save the country. The country was born death from the get-go. Education-wise—most went to school, but it is not enough to lead. The surrounding environment– most of these people have cattle keeper mindset, and the war created multicultural people who spoke different languages, making it difficult to centralize. I admit that these challenges are fundamental and need people to deal with them accordingly. The starting point in any situation is to assess the problem and examine existing issues.

What was supposed to happen before and after independence from Sudan?

Was South Sudan ready for independence?

South Sudan's only plan was separation from Sudan, but governing was another game because, with no experience whatsoever, failure was predictable. Lack of vision; the country had no plan after independence. In addition, there was a lack of proper governing, including implementation and execution.

Reforming South Sudan's national military was a massive failure from the start. Failure to establish a sense of nationality; Loyal to land, not leaders. Additionally, the naming of the country: The name 'Sudan' should not even be associated with the new country because it reminded people of the crime that was committed against the South.

New a goal, not just separation: The separation caused a few to misunderstand the history of Sudan, and unity could be achieved based on equality

The solution could be to establish a strong constitution that could save future struggles of both the North and the South.

South Sudan has universities without a textbook or curriculum. Those schools are cubs gathering, not educational institutions.

Failure in the education system now will have an indignant result and negative impact on the future generation

South Sudan's Problem

South Sudan's problem is not different from the African continent's problem. The mindset of many countries is that if you are within the African continent, then you are an African. Still, if you are outside, you are an enemy of the people.

Because the leaders fear making changes that will improve South Sudan, each suffers from the same issue. Those who work for the leaders, not citizens of the country, appoint unqualified people. This is corruption, but in some cases, these practices and norms of appointment are based on friendship.

The solution is up to all citizens of South Sudan, and the resolution should be a long-term plan with a clear vision. They should begin with the straightforward question, what does a good country look like? What are the elements of a good government? Have you ever wondered why most African countries' governments are republics' political systems?

There is no hope of the war ending soon; South Sudan was born in 2011 after the worst civil war between the North and the South. The year 2011 was a year of hope and a new chapter in the life of many people, but it wasn't long until they entered another war—the war that destroyed human assets. Today, people still live in refugee camps worldwide, including in South Sudan, which tells you how bad things are. The war created endless suffering and worries as peace and stability became an unachievable dream. Additionally, the South Sudan crises result from leadership and morals rejection within the society; and these are negatively affecting the country's future.

The Duty And Obligation Citizenship Form

Not all of us know our country's responsibility, role, duty, and obligation— citizen and government responsibility assessment form. And the leader that failed their nation should be considered a crime against their citizens.

The world could be a better, peaceful, and safe place for all humanity if each individual performs their role in good faith as a citizen. Each person in the society must have a citizenship form laying out objectives and obligations toward the community. The citizenship form should list all individual responsibilities, skills, experiences, and knowledge as well as what it can do in its ability and what the government can do for them. And to find out if you contribute to your community, you should list your skills on a scale of 0-5, where zero is the lowest. As you list your skills, you will soon discover the areas in your life that require improvement, and this will give you a big picture of whether the government is providing premises services. Local government representatives should educate their citizens and provide them with the necessary tools to improve their lives. South Sudan and the educational system. Today, South Sudan has an educational system that leads to failure. Education is obligatory for the nation's advancement, and qualified universities are necessary. I searched for South Sudan universities out of 500 universities in Africa; you cannot find one name on the list, which is sad. Putting the right people in charge is vital for designing an educational path that meets today's needs. South Sudan is in a state of critical social and is about to collapse, and their education is in the emergency room; only God knows the solution.

CHAPTER 9

HOW FAR I HAVE COME UP TO THIS POINT IN MY LIFE'S JOURNEY

Up to this point, my life is a sum of all the batter and worse experiences. It has been up and down, like the season cycle—where a season begins and ends before another season starts. It has been an uneasy journey up until this moment. My parents gave me life so I could have a future, which I'm grateful for. Leaving my parents at the beginning of 1985 was also the end of our togetherness. I gained life, and they gained death forever; we will never meet again. I lived as an orphan all the time that I spent in North Sudan but was unaware of my orphan status. I left my hometown when I was between the ages of 13 and 16. My parents died when I was away; I didn't know when my mother passed away and if I would be considered an orphan at that age. I was busy becoming someone and hoping that the war would end one day, so I could go back to my family, but that did not happen. Recently, I realized that I was living in the orphan category even though it was not spelled out.

I lived every day, asking myself why they were killing us, but finding the correct answers was impossible. My life was a journey without a map. It was a journey of fear of death, not knowing that death is gravity that you cannot escape from it. I never understood why, and God knows, and I will not bother myself because life is a stupid journey. Whoever created life or invented it fell short of showing its intentions. As long I cannot change the death outcome, it is unworthy to pursue the reason behind existing of life. My job is to seek what I will change or improve and benefit from it. Interestingly, all of us—rich, poor, weak, and robust—wait for our death or move into an unaware stage of life.

My job on earth is to live purposely to my ability before the end of my soul parts from the physical body. Interestingly, we are uncertain when and where the soul will depart the physical body and end up creating fear and confusion within our world. For this reason, if there is a God, His intentions might be different from our perceptions and understanding. My expectations of life are remarkable, but the reality of our world does not move in the same direction as mine.

In my experience, each person lives according to his aims or goals. Because each of us uniquely creates our goals with needs and values, the differences birth conflicts. We see life from a different angle in how we relate to one another. Therefore, the energy responds according to the dependences on the individual's desire. Fear death and know what to expect if you are not fully living life right now. The result could be associated with uncertainty in future life. Humans are facing challenges and conflicts everywhere in the world. Even I left as if the creator gives everyone everything to live comfortably, but we mismanage these gifts.

The feeling of freedom is good.

Your thought choices matter. When you are not free, you are already dead. I cannot say enough about the importance of freedom to think and choose what you want to be. Your choice makes you a unique individual and allows you to shape your life from your thought production. Living in the North was death itself. The country does not care about its citizens as long as they do not believe in God, and the crimes were committed in broad daylight. The mistakes of the 21st century; mistakes are mistakes, whether against individuals or groups. Have you ever wondered if it is an excellent time to be born now, before, or later in the future? What reasons are your answers based on?

Life and happiness are not stand-alone features.

The life and happiness of an individual are not stand-alone features; instead, they are rooted in many elements, from the relationship to career, to their field of study. These elements build personality and lifestyle and relate to others (relatives and close friends). Therefore, we need supportive aspects in our life. My first experience was in 1991 when I was in middle school (second year), and I was ahead of A, B, and C classes for final year results. My school was one of the three middle schools for the southerners or displaced people from the South. I was studying hard, hoping that the war would end soon, so I could go back to my parents and show them what I have done for myself. One evening, when we were leaving the school, my teacher called me into her office and asked me to dress up well the next day because the results would be announced tomorrow, and I was ahead of the second-year classes.

It was a sad day in my life. As I was preparing that night for the next day, I remembered that my parents would not be there with me. None of them will see my result, except my mates from school. My teacher introduced me to the school that evening as a quiet, intelligent, and respectful student, but these words sent a wrong signal to my mind. I received the result and could not stop crying, and nobody knew why; some were asking if I was crying because I didn't expect to be first in class. They were wrong. I wanted to be first, and it was my mission, but I was burning inside because I was missing supportive elements in my life. What was missing was showing my results at home; this was what I went through all my entire educational journey. No one will see my school reports till I leave this life; none of my parents will know about my educational journey. I was facing life alone because the devil had taken my parents away., but I was not in court to sue the enemy. Where is justice, and where will it come from? And where is God? I am powerless, and the enemy is laughing. Imagine that for a second, you can see the person who kills your father, mother three brothers, but you can't do anything. What is the meaning of life? It is hard to think my parents are gone forever and no one can be held countable for the crime.

If you think surviving the war in the South would make me happy, then you are wrong. Life needs the elements that give and support to sense the meaning of life, but the war wiped out my happiness.

Who is to blame for this mess?

Let me ask you a question, hoping it will make sense to you. If you are an engineer, and you design a tower building, put all your engineering skills into it, and then recommend all materials to build the tower. To whom does the building refer?

The world is God's image.

Before you can make a judgment go through the article?

I am not a sociologist.

Assume you did everything right, but the outcome didn't satisfy you or meet your expectation.

Who influences you negatively or positively in your social status today?

Who to blame for your failure?

Think deep—a week, or a year, even.

List all the possible entries that may have had a hand in human crises.

Have you ever asked these questions?

How much freedom do I have?

Who controls society?

What do I contribute to society?

What is my objection to society?

Is there an obligation to help others, and why?

Does God concern Himself with the world? If yes, what part?

Sometimes, you have to stop and ask yourself hard questions.

What are things you cannot afford not to talk about in this moment of your life?

- Marriage
- Education
- Career
- Family
- Government

Things that control you

- Life's road map
- Inventory—life's account register

And I am not offering answers. Instead, I am asking questions that you should ask yourself. Every story has a beginning and an end, and life is one of them.

Therefore, your life is a reflection of an untold inner story about you.

Your life begins with your date of birth. From that moment onward, you navigate society to find a way in.

In any dark journey, we see that the destination depends on belief, society's awareness, and level of education – our prediction relies on experiences that support our courage system.

Before I left the South, which is my hometown, I was nobody—in terms of responsibility. I was nobody because I had four brothers ahead of me and was allowed to go around to my uncle and aunt's houses. All my father's three sisters were married, and that was his source of wealth. I grew up with no concern about who to marry whatsoever. What was important was to have cattle and follow the tribe norm, which had simple rules. But what was more important was the family reputation; having a reputation in Jieng tribe culture is more essential than having a cattle—to marry, you need to be from a good family and have good relatives.

When I left my birthplace in early 1985

Fear and, at the same time, the desire to live made me depart from my family, and both were genuine reasons. Even when I was under the enemy's mercy, my soul and physical lived in separate worlds. I was missing my parents so bad. Sadly, they all died without me seeing them again. I was in the second grade when I left my hometown, and I was able to continue my education; I even enrolled in a college in Sudan but did not complete it. As I continued the journey to the USA, I acquired both a BS and MS and I attended a Ph.D. program. I have achieved what my parent wanted; they wanted me to survive the war and have a future. The beginning of my life in North Sudan was a dark road. I was helpless from the unknown to come, and I couldn't see the end ahead of me at all. The hope and desire to have my family with me grew stronger every day. I wanted my parents to be alive and be beside me.

However, this phrase kept me alive, "Only you can help you." This sentence helped me; this came as a life assessment, and I came to realize that no one can help me except me. When I sum up these experiences, I am only fighting for my existence. If not, I will become nothing—and I refused to be anything other than human, just like others that the provider intended to be. I always tell myself, "You have a message to the world and news," and I have to. So, I've been pushing forward and fighting for years just to find a small space and be human again.

Up to this point, my life journey was driven by hope and the expectation that tomorrow would be better.

Success is on the way; I see the light from afar, but I know it is reachable. Giving up is not in my life dictionary, and success is what I've set my mind to. Following others, I will be the rule of the road, now and for the rest of my life. I refuse to be poor—materially, mentally, and education-wise.

My mission is to remove all elements that always prevent me from achieving my goals.

I always find a reason that keeps me moving forward in life, and that is what has led me to where I am today. In my experience, I have learned that happiness and success are not destinations or points you arrive at to celebrate your achievements, but instead, it is where you're standing in the moment and seeing how far you've come.

It points to where you can start the next journey forward. Remember that the hand of the clock is always moving forward, and the wise move to get next station time never goes backward.

WOW, I am successful.

Success is mainly tied to comparison as a unit of measurement. Whether in reality or in your conscious mind, you are referencing the thing that exists now or existed in your life experiences.

We might have a different view about success, but it is the result and feelings about results or closeness to desire. Success is a location or area within self-awareness and acceptance of expectation. Also, you might be aware that the elements of success are areas within that fall and meet outcomes, events, community, or society. Success is location and time. Success is relative to locations tied to the community or society. What is the percentage?

My success unit of measure references these years; 1985, 1992, and 1996. Each of these gives unpleasant events like no other in my life.

When I left my parent and birthplace, I thought my life had lost its meaning.

My education journey almost ended in 1992, and school was the only hope I had. I could not afford not to go to school; education was the only thing I could give to my family. But unfortunately, my exam result was 208 out of 250 points, so I could not get admission into the top boarding school. The school takes only the top ten students from displaced schools or Southern students, and 208 points put me far behind, among the first 20s. The problem was that no one would be willing to support me if I went to a public high school. In 1996, before I left Sudan University of Science and Technology, electrical engineering was my dream field. But later, as a young boy, I became more interested in electrical or physics studies. These were the two career paths that I was dreaming of spending my life in. So again, I thought no more life for me anywhere in the world. I felt that was the end of the road. Looking back, success is not where or when but how you have named it.

I am thriving on my terms, and only I can help me.

CHAPTER 10

THE END

I't's been a long ride. First, I appreciate you for making it this far with me. If you are reading the last chapter of the book, chances are you're either searching for more information or falling in love with my story. For whatever reason, I am grateful to have shared my story with you. My account is just like any other story in the world. But the main reason for sharing my story is that I do not believe in war to bring about peace; because it never achieves real intent. War divides people, and both parties who engage in it will lose lives, making the winning of the war pointless.

By now, I hope you have learned something. As I mentioned in the beginning, the book focuses on three areas: My childhood, life experiences, and lessons I have learned on my life journey. I was born in a small town, which is now the capital of an oil-rich region (South Sudan). Even with its resources, the city is still struggling and at war because of political disagreement. My experience created a lens through which I view the world today and influence others' attitudes and beliefs. Leaving my family behind in early 1985 because of the civil war was a new chapter of my life. The journey was an emergency exit, and I have never returned to my birthplace. I lost my parents and three brothers in the war. One of my older brothers was killed after South Sudan's independence in 2011. I experienced a lot as I navigated through cities; from the east - Africa to the west - the United States of America. Many questions that never depart from me are whether life still has meaning and if happiness is worth pursuing? Even the South saw the light of freedom, but things did not change much as expected.

My existence and meaning of life were recreated from my association with others.

Living life, for now, is what I can do.

Is there a benefit to my existence? And will it be notable now or after my death? In war, there is no winner because both parties lose something valuable, be it human lives or properties. I can tell you about a person who lost five loved ones in the conflict. War should not be the first solution to resolving a disagreement or dispute. Like any war, clashes leave behind sad stories for both sides (the winner and the loser) of the competition. During the war, there was no communication except with the government. I did not know when my parents died and when my other two brothers were killed; I left the country in 2005 before the peace between the South and North Sudan. The conflict between North and South led to division, but this was not surprising because of political, religious, and cultural differences.

Refusal To Be Weak In My Soul

In my experiences, war leaves a trail behind (death and sadness) in your life forever, though some might celebrate a war victory. I am sharing my story to inspire young children or adults so they can have hope. Even if you see no way out, believe that you can make it with little help— even without parents or loved ones. It is vital that you focus in order to make it through the struggles. It will not be an easy journey or straight line, but you can get there safely. Be hopeful, even if it seems impossible. When I look back on my life, I cannot believe I've made it this far. I left my town with nothing, and I didn't even know where I was going, but each step I took led me to a new place, and that created a desire to continue—the future is ahead.

In my journey, I hoped that one day, things would change for the better. The trip was full of ups and downs; you believed in God one day, and the next day, you don't. In one of the previous chapters, I told you that my childhood was promising. We had food and other things that made living joyful; until the war broke out. Also, my tribe norms and culture were Jieng standards, but after the war, I went through many experiences with cultural changes; and as of now, I can call myself multicultural.

My birthplace

I was born in Pariang town; it is closer to North Sudan and is the state where most of the oil of South Sudan comes from. Pariang is the wealthiest and poorest city at the same time. Even up to this moment, no one knows where the oil money goes. People are still suffering. My childhood was promising because my parents had enough to fulfill our needs. Life was simple; the Jieng tribe depended mostly on cattle rearing and farming. The lands are packed with natural resources that do not require technical skill or machinery equipment. Life experiences throughout my beautiful childhood shaped me to become who I am today.

My journey was better and worse simultaneously; it allowed me to see the World as its and took the fear away Forever. We will be the third world-class until we change our thinking. What you get in life is what you see in the real world and not in your imagination. What everyone has is their vision that has been brought to light. Your world is given to you by the power of your imagination. You can go to the moon when you believe it. We can go to the moon without help from others, and that day, our people will have their independence. Most African countries are dependent on aids because of poor leadership, lack of imagination, and poor thinking—their way of thinking creates poverty instead of wealth and knowledge.

The City I Love

You are the only thought I have in mind.
You are the only one who can understand it.
I have never felt this way before.
Let us build a beautiful house where the love will be residing in.
From now on, you and I equal one body.
I invited you into my heart.
Let us be together tonight and forever; we will not be apart.

Because I want you in the most exact word of love, I will take care of your heart.

Nothing before or after you will replace you.

You are the only thought I have in mind.

I hope you can understand me.

I'm just thinking about you all day.

Let us be together today & forever.

Wur Deng Aeek

My Tribe

I am a Dinka (Jieng tribe). We believe in God, except that God is above.

A country that came out of war but entered into another conflict with itself.

Journey of fear

My Life And Journey Of Fear

From the start, my life was a journey without direction. It was a journey of fear from death; there was no other route to take to skip death's gravity. Life is a stupid ride, and I have never understood it; God knows I will not bother to understand it because whoever created or invented life fell short in showing his/her intentions. For a long time, I could not change the deadly consequences. I felt it was not worth pursuing the reason behind life or death's existence. My job is to seek ways through which I will be able to change or improve the lives of others during my time on earth—before the end of my soul's energy.

For this reason, if there is a God, He might be in different forms and for other desires. According to desires, beliefs, and expectations, God can be seen in various states. Therefore, responses may be different accordingly. Even in this uncertain journey, the hope and expectation that the sun would rise tomorrow and that success was on my way were the fuel that kept me going. I will see the light of freedom. Giving up has never been in my life's dictionary, and that, as a mindset, has been a tool in my life. My mission is to remove all elements that prevent me from achieving my goals.

Education.

When I left my birthplace, I was in the second grade; I was able to continue school in the long evening while working in the morning until I was accepted into high school in 1992. High school was in the morning, which meant I couldn't work in the mornings. As a result, my education journey almost came to an end. I wanted to be a full-time student, so I could focus on my education and get good grades to go to university. I was admitted to Sudan University of Science and Technology school of engineering in 1995/1996, but I did not complete it. I immigrated to the United States in 2004 and started all over again. I received my Associate's Degree in 2010, BS in 2013, and MS in 2015. I attended Capella University for a Doctor of Information Technology degree in 2016-2018 but did not graduate.

The Day Will Come

The day will come, and you will realize I am not your enemy.
One day you will learn the language of beauty and the language of love.
One day the sun of freedom will shine on us all.
Let us live together.
Let us love one another.
We are all result of the power that creates and provides a soul equally.

We are all result of our parents, whether we intended or accidentally found in an explanatory event, as there are a million reasons to get married and million reasons a man and a woman have sex. Imagine you were there the night the two (your parents) started conversing, then decided to continue the conversation outside, and then they later walked back inside. Things felt right, and then it turned physical—complete that thought. We all have a past event, whether you were born before or after marriage, that is still not a reason for someone to kill you.

War And Willingness To Live

We had the willingness to live during the war, but both God and the world were in deep silence or turned away from us. The will to live was the root of my fear; as a young boy, I wanted to live and see more of the world. Also, there was no reason not to die, and our only hope was God, as the threat and chance of death got too close. To be alive was the only thing I desired, even though I didn't know where help would come from, especially when the government was doing the killing. We were civilians without weapons to face the enemy; our lives were in danger, and God was nowhere to save us. Sudan's civil war revealed humans' dark side. It was the worst conflict Africa has ever seen; millions of people died as both God, and the world turned a deaf ear to our cries. The war partly has religious aspects, which is exposing and forcing the people to accept the religion. The goal was to make South Sudan a spiritual gateway to Africa for the introduction to Arabicization. I wanted to live with my lovely parents and brothers, but God was nowhere to be found. In early 1984, the Sudan - Arabic government attacked cities and villages in South Sudan. The unbalancing power between the North and the South was not to be compared, and only God could help, especially when we didn't have any weapons to fight the enemy. And the unavoidable question is, what part of human life does God protect or is He concerned about? The safety of the human soul should be the core center of God's existence, especially when death comes unwillingly. There was no food or water, and the world and God were far enough to offer help to the people of South Sudan. And what I have come to learn and experience is that the fact that we are simply black, we do not deserve to live or even enjoy our human rights. Dreaming of a peaceful society and city of angels cannot be achieved now or forever as long as others still have different agendas toward other human beings. Even in these challenges, I refuse to be a slave or poor in the soul. Because you, me, and everyone else are here by the same channel that imagined everything into existence. I am a billionaire in my soul, and I have in abundance. Also, I am of higher quality in my human attribute. Therefore, I will not be under your control today or in the future. But we could build a peaceful city where we can all live together and have the same right.

The Journey Last Notes

Success and failure.

Success and failure are concepts and means used to measure society's progress and classifications. No one is a success or failure. These concepts are only used to describe different things that exist when no other fact exists at that moment. You can't tell who the poorest person in the world is, but you can tell who the richest person in the world is.

Let's look at the following points.

- Beauty
- Tall
- Short
- Rich
- Poor
- Father
- Mother

To live is an act of courage and determination, not luck or a wish. Remember, life is a journey of uncertainty to an unknown destination. We aspire to find the right path that will lead us to imaginary comfortable bus stops. Interestingly, success and failure are parallel lines that go in the same direction and are invisible to most. Success or failure is an internal condition that is, ideally, tools driven by society's progression. In a sense, the idea of living successfully or unsuccessfully is how you see others internally or how others see you. This can be found within individual assessments of oneself. Concisely, we all report to the whole world—just like you see on social media today. Unaware, we submit a report about our life status to our immediate community or society as a whole.

Role And Responsibility

Each individual has a role and responsibility toward the community and society they live in.

Africans' future begins with everyone's contribution.

Part of the African problem can be traced to many roots—weather, environment, language, lack of effective government system, lack of vision, and religion.

These are some of the factors that contribute to Africa's condition. The desire to better Africa will begin by repainting the African image to the African children.

The first step is valuing yourself as a black person. We have to trust ourselves and love the relationship between ourselves as black people.

Self-love is critical to curing the past.

Self-discovery is a healing guide to better Africa.

You cannot give what you do not have in your own capacity.

The past has shadowed my thoughts up until this point.

The Past That Followed My Thoughts

History records all our past experiences—good and bad. Interestingly, we store some for an extended period of time. Some of the experiences we let go of are of the past. My life, in the beginning, was promising until it turned upside down. I have experienced a lot and struggled so much; these experiences shadowed my thoughts every day and took away the joy in my life. These experiences stand as a divider between the past, the present, and the future. I struggled to let go of the past because I continually followed the trail left behind by the shadow of history. My memories are dark shadows that follow me wherever I go. But despite the unthinkable past, I decided to be happy happiness is a gift that I could afford without cost.

There Will Always Be A Choice.

There will always be a choice to make in life

Silence is a choice.

And I choose to be silent

If there is dark, there is no light,

If there is war, there is no peace,

And I prefer light over dark

And peace over war

There is always a choice to make in life.

I choose hope over fear

I prefer Happiness over sadness

There is always a choice to make in life.

There is always a choice to make in life.
And I choose to be silent
I choose love over hate
I prefer a friendship over being an enemy
I was born to be a leader, not a follower
I was born to be greater, not less than others
I was born to be wise, not to be ignorant
I was told I am not who I am
But I say you are fucking ignorant
Neither you nor God can stop me from being happy
There is always a choice to make in life
But I choose to be silent
I chose love
I chose Peace
I chose wisdom
I choose Joy
I chose Happiness
There is always a choice to make in life
And I choose to be silent
Silence
Silence
Silence

Printed in Great Britain
by Amazon